Date Due

3LYAUG01			

BRODART, INC.   Cat. No. 23 233   Printed in U.S.A.

PRICE: $16.99 (3559/he)

BOOKS BY DON MCKAY

Air Occupies Space 1973
Long Sault 1975
Lependu 1978
Lightning Ball Bait 1980
Birding, or desire 1983
Sanding Down This Rocking Chair on a Windy Night 1987
Night Field 1991
Apparatus 1997
Another Gravity 2000

ANOTHER GRAVITY

Don McKay

CANADIAN CATALOGUING IN PUBLICATION DATA

McKay, Don, 1942-
    Another gravity

ISBN 0-7710-5764-4

I. Title.

PS8575.K28A76 2000   c811'.54   C99-933000-4
PR9199.3.M45A76 2000

We acknowledge the financial support of the Government of Canada through the Book Publishing Industry Development Program for our publishing activities. We further acknowledge the support of the Canada Council for the Arts and the Ontario Arts Council for our publishing program.

Typeset in Aldus by M&S, Toronto
Printed and bound in Canada

McClelland & Stewart Inc.
The Canadian Publishers
481 University Avenue
Toronto, Ontario
M5G 2E9

1 2 3 4 5   04 03 02 01 00

CONTENTS

ONE

Sometimes a voice – have you heard this? –
wants not to be voice any longer, wants something
whispering between the words, some
rumour of its former life. Sometimes, even
in the midst of making sense or conversation, it will
hearken back to breath, or even farther,
to the wind, and recognize itself
as troubled air, a flight path still
looking for its bird.
                  I'm thinking of us up there
shingling the boathouse roof. That job is all
off balance – squat, hammer, body skewed
against the incline, heft the bundle,
daub the tar, squat. Talking,
as we always talked, about not living
past the age of thirty with its
labyrinthine perils: getting hooked,
steady job, kids, business suit. Fuck that. The roof
sloped upward like a take-off ramp
waiting for Evel Knievel, pointing into open sky. Beyond it
twenty feet or so of concrete wharf before
the blue-black water of the lake. Danny said
that he could make it, easy. We said
never. He said case of beer, put up
or shut up. We said
asshole. Frank said first he should go get our beer
because he wasn't going to get it paralysed or dead.
Everybody got up, taking this excuse

to stretch and smoke and pace the roof
from eaves to peak, discussing gravity
and Steve McQueen, who never used a stunt man, Danny's
life expectancy, and whether that should be a case
of Export or O'Keefe's. We knew what this was –
ongoing argument to fray
the tedium of work akin to filter vs. plain,
stick shift vs. automatic, condom vs.
pulling out in time. We flicked our butts toward the lake
and got back to the job. And then, amid the squat,
hammer, heft, no one saw him go. Suddenly he
wasn't there, just his boots
with his hammer stuck inside one like a heavy-headed
flower. Back then it was bizarre that,
after all that banter, he should be so silent,
so inward with it just to
run off into sky. Later I thought,
cool. Still later I think it makes sense his voice should
sink back into breath and breath
devote itself to taking in whatever air
might have to say on that short flight between the roof
and the rest of his natural life.

LIFT

To stand with mind akimbo where the wind
riffles the ridge. Slow,
slow jazz: it must begin
before the instrument with bones
dreaming themselves hollow and the dusk
rising in them like a sloth
ascending. Moon,
night after night rehearsing shades of pause
and spill, sifting into reed beds,
silvering the fine hairs on your arms, making
rhythm out of light and nothing, making
months. What have I ever made of life or it
of me? All I ever asked for
was to be remembered constantly
by everything I ever touched.
                              Now I need
a scrap of night to wrap up in and sleep who
knows how many eons until something –
maybe dotted, maybe ragged,
maybe dun – unfolds. Something quick.
Something helpful to the air.

DRAG

But, however,
on the other hand.
Not gravity, that irresistible embrace,
but its photograph, packed in your bag
with too many shirts. Drag
wants to dress the nakedness of speed, to hold clothes
in the slipstream until body reincarnates, then
it will be sorry, won't it?
Yes it will. It will be as sorry as the
square of its upward urge.
                    When I approached the edge
it seemed one gentle waft
would carry me across, the brief lilt
of a Horned Lark up from roadside gravel
into the adjacent field.
                    However,
on the other hand. It occurred to me that,
unlike Horned Larks, who are imagination,
I was mostly memory, which,
though photogenic and nutritious, rich
with old-time goodness, is notoriously
heavier than air.

DARK OF THE MOON

Once past the street lights I miss it,
"poised" at the spruce tip, "floating"
in the pond, the way it gathered longing into moths
and kept reality from overdosing on its own sane
self. It seems the dead,
who would otherwise be dressing up in moonstuff, blending
with the birch to be both here
and not here, lose interest in us and descend
below the reach of roots. The hydro wires
are hydro wires, the streets are streets, the houses
full of television. On tombstones
names and dates are fading into vague
depressions, or else (not impossibly)
we have forgotten how to read. Who can say
if these are names or simply the effect
of weather on the stone, and if they were,
what possible connection they would have to persons
rumoured to have once gone to and fro? No one,
says Yeats, but no one
is born at this phase, whose only
incarnation is the dark. Possibly this is the hole
the Fool (phase 28) falls into –
                              so I reflect as,
taking the path among the evergreens,
I lose my way – the way I know like the back
of my own hand – which is busy fending off
the clutchings of the spruce – the very spruce I planted
forty years ago – and wind up

besnaggled in the dark and many-needled wood
which is mythless
which is pathless
which is mine.

SONG FOR THE SONG OF THE COYOTE

Moondogs, moondogs,
tell me the difference between tricks
and wisdom, hunting
and grieving.
I listen in the tent, my ear
to the ground. There is a land even
more bare than this one, without sage,
or prickly pear, or greasewood. A land
that can only wear its scars, every crater
etched. Riverless. Treeless. You sing to its thin
used-up light, yips and floated tremolos and screams,
sculpted barks like fastballs of packed
air. Echoes that articulate the buttes and coulees and dissolve
into the darkness, which is always listening.

LOAD

We think this
the fate of mammals – to bear, be born,
be burden, to carry our own bones
as far as we can and know the force that earths us
intimately. Sometimes, while I was reading,
Sam would bestow one large paw on my foot,
as if to support my body
while its mind was absent – mute
commiseration, load to load, a message
like the velvet heaviness which comes
to carry you deliciously
asleep.
            One morning
on the beach at Point Pelee, I met
a White-throated Sparrow so exhausted from the flight
across Lake Erie it just huddled in itself
as I crouched a few yards off.
I was thinking of the muscles in that grey-white breast,
pectoralis major powering each downstroke,
pectoralis minor with its rope-and-pulley tendon
reaching through the shoulder to the
top side of the humerus to haul it up again;
of the sternum with the extra keel it has evolved to
anchor all that effort, of the dark wind
and the white curl on the waves below, the slow dawn
and the thickening shoreline.

                                  I wanted
very much to stroke it, and recalling
several terrors of my brief
and trivial existence, didn't.

TWO

BEFORE THE MOON

was a moon,
before it fisted itself into otherness inside the
body of the earth, bulbed,
broke out on its own,
there was no second gravity and no
dark art of reflection. The sun owned
all the media and it occurred to no one to resist
its health-and-fitness
propaganda. Whatever a thing was,
that was it, no ifs or
airspace. Place was obese
before the moon was moon, so full of itself
there was no leaving home, and so
no dwelling in it either. Longing was short
and sedentary. Blues were red. No sweet tug
toward our manic possibilities, no wistful,
sidelong, inner, sly, no alder branch
hung above the smooth rush of the snow-fed river like the
stray wisp hovering against your cheek which
in a moment you will tuck back
into tidiness, no such stretched connection before
moon was moon. No way to deflect the light
away from photosynthesis and into alcohol
and film. Each night
was the same night, and fell formlessly,
with no imagination,
and without you in it.

ANGLE OF ATTACK

You may openly
endorse the air, but if you can't
be canny, and, come to that, apt,
chances are you won't
get off the ground.
                We audited
our raw materials: a lawn chair,
an abandoned stroller, and a snarl
of coat hangers – necks, hooks, elbows –
wrangling. Handles and
clock hands. How-to's on migration guided
by the stars, by the earth's
electromagnetism, by the ultra-low groans
spoken by the mountains. Now
we needed duct tape, a philosophy of feathers
and a plan: what to
fall for, gracefully,
and without too much
deliberation, how to mix
the mysticism with the ash and live
next door to nothing,
and with art.

FOREST MOON

(June: Williamstown, Ontario)

The light, though full of motion,
neither falls nor pours
into the clearing, but as it enters, ebbs
back into itself:
                              we float off from the porch,
letting its tug entice us
to the path. What used to be basswood leaves
are silver gloves that beckon,
this way, this way,
down to the abandoned tracks.
The old rails,
who spend their days becoming rust,
are glimmering with distance, tracks left
by some ardent creature we have just missed seeing.
Fortunately.
                        Where can they be pointing?
Not to Cornwall, Ontario.
Not to any place I'd care to put a name to.

as it becomes the wolf who howls into its windless
drift, soul
into solitude. If you want
to carry it home in a jar, a sort of superior
propane for the stoves and fridges of the arts, it simply
swims into the wish and
spikes it. It becomes you. It reads you
backward, turning the pages softly but coldly, this one
which is heavy with names and this one
sticky with praise and this one which is the pane
you see through to unbind the book. Not
that it dissolves its hosts but that it wakes them to an
inner drinking, something
seeking the sea, something that leaves them larger
and less.

HOMING

That things should happen
twice, and place
share the burden of remembering. Home,
the first cliché. We say it
with aspiration as the breath
opens to a room of its own (a bed,
a closet for the secret self), then closes
on a hum. Home. Which is the sound of time
braking a little, growing slow and thick as the soup
that simmers on the stove. Abide,
abode. Pass me that plate,
the one with the hand-painted *habitant*
sitting on a log. My parents bought it
on their honeymoon – see? Dated on the bottom,
1937. He has paused to smoke his pipe, the tree
half cut and leaning. Is he thinking where
to build his cabin or just idling his mind
while his pipe smoke mingles with the air? A bird,
or something (it is hard to tell), hangs overhead.
Now it's covered by your grilled cheese sandwich.

Part two, my interpretation. The leaning tree
points home, then
past home into real estate and its innumerable
Kodak moments: kittens, uncles,
barbecues. And behind those scenes the heavy
footstep on the stair, the face locked
in the window frame, things that happen

and keep happening, reruns
of family romance. And the smudged bird? I say it's
a Yellow Warbler who has flown
from winter habitat in South America to nest here
in the clearing. If we catch it, band it,
let it go a thousand miles away it will be back
within a week. How?
Home is what we know
and know we know, the intricately
feathered nest. Homing
asks the question.

RUNNING AWAY

I was four
and leaving Cornwall,
Ontario, for a life at sea. What

possessed me? Not the effects
of the Howard Smith Paper Mill's emissions on my
innocent sinus passages, nor the H-bomb,

nor the arrival of my younger brother
and the sudden fall from myth
to politics and history. I blame

Little Tim and the Brave Sea Captain, whose
watercolour illustrations led the eye along the sweet
curl of the waves and the Brave

Sea Captain's pipe smoke into the wide-
open page where who
knew what. Later,

force-fed *Heart of Darkness* I would recognize
the mute tug of that empty space
inside the map of Africa, rendered in Conrad's

Latin-heavy hand. Little Tim
called this adventure.
I was afraid of it and so

I had to go. My companion and bad influence
a spaniel named Sam, whose blond
muzzle and eyebrows made him look a little

like an Evening Grosbeak and a lot like Groucho Marx,
but wiser, as befits a dog. Off
we went to the canal, which ran

the length of town and would,
as I inferred, precociously, from *Paddle-to-the-Sea*,
take me to the ocean. Often,

after Sunday School, I was taken to watch ships rise
or fall as they passed through the locks.
Now filled in,

grassed over, that whole canal's a park
the city can be proud of. Then it was the place
where mechanism met the river, dangerous

and dirty. Perfect. Kids were always,
I was told, falling off the edge and getting drowned
or mashed between the ship that slowly

and majestically rose and the slick
wall of the lock. I see Sam and my small self
following its hard line, watching for a fuzzy

watercolour ship or a sailor with a certain curl
to smoke or smile. What kind of film is this, I wonder,
some *Lassie Come Home* spinoff or a grim

grainy documentary in which the figures are about
to fade into the screen's amnesia? In my viewfinder
the kid's head is a piece of empty sky, an afternoon

with high cloud moving in. Sam glances sideways, one
blond eyebrow raised. His fate was to be always
on the verge of speech, full of the rich

paradoxes of domestic life and wildness, just about
to clue us in before he realized afresh
how deaf we were. In later years

he'd dig a passage underneath the fence
to liberate my little brother from the back yard,
lead him, toddling,

across several busy streets to wind up
contemplating traffic from a stranger's porch.
Later still

he'd sleep whole days away lying
in the middle of the road and finally,
one Hallowe'en, he stretched out on the lawn

and died, and never spoke a word.
But it was Sam
who tipped them off. Someone spotted him

by the canal and phoned my frantic parents.
What possessed me? Did I realize
they'd called the police, did

I know what that meant? *Jail.* The word "adventure"
failed to calm them. I did not mention
that I was afraid and so

I had to go. They sent me off to bed
then got me up and fed me peanut butter sandwiches
and milk. Who knew what? No one in the story

with a speaking part. No voice
split the clouds proclaiming Woe Unto Thee, Kid,
for thy dire misdeed henceforth

shall Home forever run away from Thee. It was
1947, war was dead. Hope boomed,
reverberated and became incarnate

in the form of Dr. Spock.
It conjured heroes like Tobias from *The Book of Tobit*,
sent off on his journey with an angel

and a dog, a little model of the cosmos with the kid placed
comfily between the spirit and the beast. Like us,
that story soon forgets about its dog,

so it's the angel who ensures Tobias gets
the glory, and the money,
and the girl. A myth

for winners. For the rest of us from whom
home runs away, I call the ghost of Sam to be
the sage of vagabondage, a.k.a. the dog

in the machine. Once again to set out,
fingers buried in his fur, to give ourselves
to serendipity and follow his exquisite nose

through rich denatured air down
to the canal, to watch its strict
domestication of the river, its huge chains

dragging those gates against the water,
the tankers named for Texaco and Shell, the quick rat
and the man who yells *Hey kid*

va t'en chez toi, and the black
belly-button swirl that surfaces and winks
and disappears behind the stern of each

departing ship.

THREE

Another gravity. I am on my way
to the bathroom, the dream in my head still
struggling not to die into the air, when my bare feet step
into a pool of moonlight on the kitchen floor and turn,
effortlessly, into fish. All day surviving in the grim purdah
of my work socks wishing only to be kissed by cold
equivocal light, now they swim off,
up, singing old bone river, hunched-up toes
and gormless ankles growing
sleek and silver, old bone river,
gather me back.
On pause in my kitchen,
footless, I think of them up there among the night fliers –
Snow Geese, swans, songbirds –
navigating by the stars and earth's own
brainwaves. How early radar techs discovered
ghostly blotches on their screens and,
knowing they weren't aircraft – theirs
or ours – called them angels. Back in my dream
the old lady who sells popcorn has been fading in my arms
as I run through its corridors and lobbies, taking her
empty weight through foyers, antechambers,
vestibules, a whole aerobics class completely deaf
inside its trance of wellness, my old
popcorn lady dwindling to a feather boa,
then a scarf of smoke. A gravity
against the ground, a love
which summons no one home

and calls things to their water-souls. On the tide flats
shore birds feed and bustle, putting on fat
for the next leg of the long
throw south. When a cold front
crosses the Fundy coast, they test it
with their feathers, listening to its muscular
northwesterlies, deciding when to give their bodies
to that music and be swept,
its ideal audience, far out over the Atlantic. The face
in the bathroom mirror looks up
just as I arrive, a creature that has
caught me watching and is watching back. Around us
wind has risen, rushes in the foliage,
tugs at the house.

SNOW MOON

(January: Fredericton, New Brunswick)

With no name
and no mask. Not the dusty rock,
not the goddess, not the decor of romance,
not the face. Express from infinity
it arrives in a flood of cold desire like a
tooth, like a voracious
reader. The snow wakes singing, its empty angels
filling with invisible silica, quickening
to fly off as Snowy Owls.
The mind of winter.
                    This moon who refuses to defer,
whose light is the death of fire and the silence of the loon,
whose song can snap off ears.

KINDS OF BLUE #41 (FAR HILLS)

Viola, cello, double bass, the distances
deepen and address us. What is this language
we have almost learnt, or nearly not
forgotten, with its soft
introspective consonants, its drone
of puréed names? It says we ought to mourn
but not to grieve, it says that even loss
may be a place, it says
repose. The eye would like to fold its rainbow
like a fan, and quit
discriminating between this and that,
and indigo and mauve,
and go there. Once,
while sleeping in my down-filled sleeping bag
I dreamt of Eiders, diving
and diving into the dark Arctic Ocean, and woke
bereft and happy, my whole mind
applauding.

SONG FOR THE SONG OF THE WHITE-THROATED SPARROW

Before it can stop itself, the mind
has leapt up inferences, crag to crag,
the obvious arpeggio. Where there is a doorbell
there must be a door – a door
meant to be opened from inside.
Door means house means – wait a second –
but already it is standing on a threshold previously
known to be thin air, gawking. The Black Spruce
point to it: clarity,
melting into ordinary morning, true
north. Where the sky is just a name,
a way to pitch a little tent in space and sleep
for five unnumbered seconds.

CAMBER

That rising curve, the fine line
between craft and magic where we
travel uphill without effort, where anticipation,
slipping into eros,
                        summons the skin. When you
say "you" with that inflection something stirs
inside the word, echo
infected with laugh. One night O., gazing at the moon
as usual, encountered K. as he was trying to outwalk
bureaucracy. Yes, they said, let's. If it is
possible to translate poetry, then,
what isn't?

GLIDE

Sometimes the eye brims
over with desire and pours
into its flight path:

this is gaze, and glide
is when the body follows,
flowing into river, when the heart,

turning the word "forever"
into plainsong,
learns to purr, knowing

the most important
lesson of grade four
is the blank but pointed

page, the pure wish that we
sharpen into dart and send
skimming the desks and out

the window, through the schoolyard
with its iron jungle gym, across
the traffic we must always

stop and look both
ways for, meanwhile, gazing
at us from its prehistoric perch, a small

but enterprising lizard
is about to launch itself
into the warm arms of the Mesozoic afternoon.

HOVER

What goes up
improvises, makes itself a shelf out of nowt,
out of ether and work, ushering the air, backstroke
after backstroke, underneath
the earth turns and you
don't, and don't
and don't: O
who do you think you are so
hugely paused, pissing off both
gravity and time,
refusing to be born into the next
inexorable instant?
We wait in our
pocket of held breath:
                    do it for us.

What does the moon mean? When you can't look up at it, you can
look it up:

      mēnē (Gk.), whence menses, month, the first long
measure, the arc of time riding its slow wink past
the day-in day-out doorslams of the sun: whence

                          metre, as measure
enters the sentence, each phrase a move
that thinks of other moves, as eros, as the line may open out
or snap shut.

      Period, *peri odos*, the way around, the way
that measure makes us and we may eventually
re-pose the question, where does meaning
come from? Finding time, feeling its slow pulse, taking
place within it: *mēnē*: dimension: commensurate:
immense.

LUNA MOTH MEDITATION

How foolish to think death's pale flag
would be rectangular and stark, rather than this
scrap of wedding dress symmetrically ripped
and sent back, cruelly,
to be his deaf and nearly mouthless
messenger. As it unfolds – gorgeous, appalling –
I can feel my mind fill up
with its own weight, as though
suffering unexpected snowfall.
Think of a Eurydice who makes it
all the way, following an Orpheus
with more self-discipline,
and probably less talent, just to find herself
forbidden that huge
other eros:
            how she craves the darkness and her legs
drink down into dirt. And that moment
in the sickroom when the dead one's been removed
and the Kleenex in the waste can
starts to metamorphose, tissue
taking wing, wing
taking the very drape and slope of grief
and struggling out the door.

FOUR

isn't sorry. We do not find him
doing penance, writing out the golden mean for all
eternity, or touring its high schools to tell student bodies
not to do what he done
done. Over and over he rehearses flight
and fall, tuning his moves, entering
with fresh rush into the mingling of the air
with spirit. This is his practice
and his prayer: to be translated into air, as air
with each breath enters lungs,
then blood. He feels resistance gather in his stiff
strange wings, angles his arms to shuck the sweet lift
from the drag, runs the full length
of a nameless corridor, his feet striking the paving stones
less and less heavily, then
they're bicycling above the ground,
a few shallow beats and he's up,
he's out of the story and into the song.

At the melting point of wax, which now he knows
the way Doug Harvey knows the blue line,
he will back-beat to create a pause, hover for maybe fifty
hummingbird heartbeats and then
lose it, tumbling into freefall, shedding feathers
like a lover shedding clothes. He may glide
in the long arc of a Tundra Swan or pull up sharp
to Kingfisher into the sea which bears his name. Then,
giving it the full Ophelia, drown.

On the shore
the farmer ploughs his field, the dull ship
sails away, the poets moralize about our
unsignificance. But Icarus is thinking tremolo and
backflip, is thinking
next time with a half-twist
and a tuck and isn't
sorry.

*

Repertoire, technique. The beautiful contraptions bred from inge-
nuity and practice, and the names by which he claims them, into
which – lift-off, loop-the-loop – they seem to bloom. Icarus could
write a book. Instead he will stand for hours in that musing half-
abstracted space, watching. During fall migrations he will often
climb to the edge of a north-south running ridge where the
soaring hawks find thermals like naturally occurring laughter,
drawing his eyebeam up an unseen winding stair until they nearly
vanish in the depth of sky. Lower down, Merlins slice the air with
wings that say crisp crisp, precise as sushi chefs, while Sharp-shins
alternately glide and flap, hunting as they go, each line break
poised, ready to pivot like a point guard or Robert Creeley. Icarus
notices how the Red-tails and Broadwings separate their primaries
to spill a little air, giving up just enough lift to break their drag up
into smaller trailing vortices. What does this remind him of? He
thinks of the kind of gentle teasing that can dissipate a dark mood
so it slips off as a bunch of skirmishes and quirks. Maybe that.
Some little gift to acknowledge the many claims of drag and keep
its big imperative at bay. Icarus knows all about that one.

44

In the spring he heads for a slough and makes himself a blind out of wolf willow and aspen, then climbs inside to let the marsh-mind claim his thinking. The soft splashdowns of Scaup and Bufflehead, the dives which are simple shrugs and vanishings; the Loon's wing, thin and sharp for flying in the underwater world, and the broad wing of the Mallard, powerful enough to break the water's grip with one sweep, a guffaw which lifts it straight up into the air. Icarus has already made the mistake of trying this at home, standing on a balustrade in the labyrinth and fanning like a manic punkah, the effort throwing him back-ward off his perch and into a mock urn which the Minotaur had, more than once, used as a pisspot. Another gift of failure. Now his watching is humbler, less appropriative, a thoughtless think-ing amid fly drone and dragonfly dart. Icarus will stay in the blind until his legs cramp up so badly that he has to move. He is really too large to be a foetus for more than an hour. He unbends creakily, stretches, and walks home, feeling gravity's pull upon him as a kind of wealth.

*

Sometimes Icarus dreams back into his early days with Daedalus in the labyrinth. Then he reflects upon the Minotaur, how seldom they saw him – did they ever? – while they shifted constantly from no-place to no-place, setting up false campsites and leaving decoy models of themselves. Sometimes they would come upon these replicas in strange postures, holding their heads in their laps or pointing to their private parts. Once they discovered two sticks stuck like horns in a decoy's head, which Daedalus took to be the worst of omens. Icarus was not so sure.

For today's replay he imagines himself sitting in a corridor reflecting on life as a Minotaur (*The* Minotaur) while waiting for his alter ego to come bumbling by. They were, he realizes, both children of technology – one its *enfant terrible*, the other the rash adolescent who, they will always say, should never have been given a pilot's licence in the first place. What will happen when they finally meet? Icarus imagines dodging like a Barn Swallow, throwing out enough quick banter to deflect his rival's famous rage and pique his interest. How many Minotaurs does it take to screw in a light bulb? What did the queen say to the machine? Should he wear two sticks on his head, or save that for later? He leaps ahead to scenes out of the Hardy Boys and Tom Sawyer. They will chaff and boast and punch each other on the arm. They will ridicule the weird obsessions of their parents. As they ramble, cul-de-sacs turn into secret hideouts and the institutional corridors take on the names of birds and athletes. They discover some imperfections in the rock face, nicks and juts which Daedalus neglected to chisel off, and which they will use to climb, boosting and balancing each other until they fall off. Together they will scheme and imagine. Somehow they will find a way to put their brute heads in the clouds.

WINGS OF SONG

"We talk because we are mortal."
    – Octavio Paz

And because we aren't gods,
or close to gods,
we sing. Your breath steps
boldly into lift to feel that other breath
breathing inside it: Summertime, Amazing Grace. And when it stops
you sense that something fold back
into air to leave you listening,
lonely as a post. Shall we call this angel?
Shall we call it animal, or elf? Most of us
are happy with a brief
companionable ghost who joins us in the shower or
behind the wheel. Blue Moon, Hound Dog, Life
Is Like a Mountain Railroad. When your voice
decides to quit its day job, which is mostly
door to door, to take its little sack of sounds
and pour them into darkness, with its
unembodied barks and murmurs, its refusal
to name names, its disregard for sentences,
for getting there on time,
or getting there,
or getting.

FEATHER

The mystery of feather
is the birth of listening in the late Jurassic,
how out of ordinary hearing came this quick
attention to the air, how between those fine
aspiring lizards and the wind there was this give
and give, that thickening of nothings
into lift, and the mystery

of feather is the womb of song, inside
the strict routine of scales it stirs and
shrugs its small shoulders,
stretches its trapezoids, fingers its new
curves and the

mystery of feather is to think of an infinity of hairs like
prehistoric Velcro zipping up to catch and hold and
spill the wind and the mystery of

feather is the birth of the caress, that moment
when my skin begins to bloom toward your fingers, who are
skimming, like Sanderlings across the sand,
the incredulous articulations of my back.

HANG TIME

Some say it's the blip
produced when missing heartbeats – from the terrible half-
expected phone call or the child who wasn't where you
thought she was – sneak back into flow
and get assimilated. Some say
sunspots. Either way, evidence of eddies
in the ever-rolling stream, a gift to the wingless which
increases our capacity to yearn
and taste for tricks. You have a strange expression
on your face, as though
walking a long corridor of doors, trying each one,
1324, No Entry, 1326, one of these
has got to be the way up
to the roof.

There is at present no precise definition of turbulence, although
we can say that velocity exhibits finite oscillations of a random
character that cause irregularities in the path of a suspended par-
ticle of scale comparable with the lengths that determine the
kinematics of the mean motion, we can say
vortices
       eddies
             coefficient of drag
                         we can say agitated
particles, we can say at present no,
at present there is precious
deformation, the ferocity exhibits final
oscar nominations of those random
characters, the claws, irregulars, the plaths of suspense,
the partisans of sale, the compost rabble
and the lynx that undermines, we can say
killer statics of mean motion, dwarf diseases,
all the eds and eddies and the sad
co-fishermen of drag, the agitated
hearts and hearticles of what
we cannot say there is at present.

END-OF-SUMMER MOON

(August: Victoria, B.C.)

Earlier it rose from cloud,
waking the last wisps into a soft watercolour
halo – some delicate catastrophe
struggling from its chrysalis into flimsy
moondriven life.

But now it burns with its ancient fireless fires
calling the so-called senseless and the so-called dead.
It sheds the heart,
a rubber glove turned inside out and hung,
snakeless, from the faucet.
It elides each upward-tilted face to speak
directly to the patient architecture of the bones.
The white plastic lawn chairs,
who have never been alive,
have found the birch grove of their ghosts, light-years off
from $19.99 and Zellers.
The toaster's glance is sharp
as any slice of life.

Down the road, sounds of a party –
barks of laughter, whoops of desperate
back-to-school fun – float into its glare
to get X-rayed. For a moment
we feel sorry for the social animal

who is invertebrate and brave.
                              While in the distance
dancing the trillion names of its nothing, that monstrous
silver moonfish we call ocean.

Rogue translation. Out of lullaby and slow
cathedral air to wrench this barely
thickened sibilance and make it mean
the sudden death of sound: *hush*.
                                        So more
than silent is the flight of owls
the slightest rustle gives itself away,
conspires to perish.
The owls have struck a deal with drag, their wide wings
fringed like petticoats, the underneath
covered by a sort of nap as though
wearing frillies on the outside.
They come as a quilt,
as the softness inside touch that
whispers in your skin.
The neighbourhoods they flow through
turn into the underworld unfolding behind Orpheus as,
endlessly, he climbs toward us – the deep call
of its gravity, the frail memory of day,
the vertigo which is the cocktail of the two together
mixing in his mind: *hush*.
                            The Barred Owl swept
out of our neighbour's tree and passed
just above our heads before it vanished
into the yard across the street. And awe rose,
from what depth we could not say, and left the dusk
seduced. We turned to walk back home. What cats,
we wondered, were just then being let out,
lovingly, into the night?

UFO

Leaving home loves homing: you can scrawl that
in the washroom, carve it in the old oak, carry it
inside your carry-on
luggage. When I comprehend the tragicomic
turns and nude scenes of their long
romance it's going to explain
plenty, from the strange behaviours of the dead
to why I do the dishes happily
and badly. In the cemetery by the sea
the Chestnut-backed Chickadees kibitz and flit, Yew
to Douglas-fir to Weeping
Birch. They must be the selves
of dear departed ones, still full of just
a minute while I put the kettle on and doctors,
what do they know. Wearing their
tangibility and pluck, their fresh
capacity for being sorely missed. Wearing the way
you sang off key like a new plaid
sports coat. While those others, the cherished
and exquisite rumours of the spirit, soar through our
imaginations with the dumb nonchalance
of albatrosses. Sometimes I listen
much too closely to the crows,
especially those who perch on the neon signs
and rooftops of the plaza, where they
parley in the voices of burnt
oboes, boldface and illegible.
They know something. Something

about scavenging and shopping and the interwoven
deerpaths of desire. Something about loss
made visible. Homing loves leaving
home. When I comprehend that wing.
When I run off with that heartless music.

PLUMMET

Simple.
Under one wing you take the thousand thousand
thuds of your heart, under the other
a lifetime paying taxes to the wind –
and clench.
Where there was flibbertigibbetry of feather, now
        the quick of existence in a fist.
Where there was phrase, phrase, nickel-and-diming it to stay
one breath ahead, now
        you take the full stop in your teeth
        the plumb bob
        the bomb.
Where there were unnumbered paths of air, now
        the one shaft of your plunge, whose walls
        are the shrieks of your old nemesis, gravity

        bursting into bloom.

FIVE

SOMETIMES A VOICE (2)

Sometimes a voice – have you heard this? –
wants not to be voice any longer and this longing
is the worst of longings. Nothing
assuages. Not the curry-comb of conversation,
not the dog-eared broken
satisfactions of the blues. It huddles in the lungs
and won't come out. Not for the Mendelssohn Choir
constructing habitable spaces in the air, not for Yeats
intoning "Song of the Old Mother" to an ancient
microphone. It curls up in its cave
and will not stir. Not for the gentle quack
of saxophone, not for raven's far-calling
croak. Not for *oh* the lift of poetry, or *ah*
the lover's sigh, or *um* the phrase's lost
left shoe. It tucks its nose beneath its brush
and won't. If her whisper tries
to pollinate your name, if a stranger yells
hey kid, va t'en chez toi to set another music
going in your head it simply
enters deafness. Nothing
assuages. Maybe it is singing
high in the cirque, burnishing itself
against the rockwall, maybe it is
clicking in the stones turned by the waves like faceless
dice. Have you heard this? – in the hush
of invisible feathers as they urge the dark,
stroking it toward articulation? Or the moment

when you know it's over and the nothing which you
have to say is falling all around you, lavishly,
pouring its heart out.

FINGER POINTING AT THE MOON

"We come from a hidden ocean, and go to an unknown ocean."
  – Antonio Machado

Everything you think of has already happened
and been sung by the sea. We were hiking
along the coast, with the hush and boom of surf
in our ears, on a trail so wet it was mostly
washouts strung together, forcing us
to find fresh ways around, teetery
and nimble, until I thought, yes,
the real agenda of this so-called trail
is not to lead us through this sopping biomass
but into it, with the surf
as soundtrack. *Everything you think,* it sang,
has already happened and been sung in long
confessional sighs and softly
crashing dactyls, wash, rinse,
wash, useless to resist. Each wave,
having travelled incognito through its ocean,
surges up to rush the rock, Homer was here, and perish,
famous and forgotten. On the beach
the back-drag clicks the stones and pebbles
on each other, a death rattle that is somehow soothing, somehow
music, some drum kit from the far side of the blues
where loss begins to shuffle. It's O.K. to disappear. Off balance,
I'm trying to hop from stepping stone to stone
when I flash back forty years to my friend's
younger sister sitting in the boat,

trailing her fingers as we row out to the raft, how she gazes,
pouring herself into water as its depth
pours into her. I remember
being embarrassed she'd been caught out
having an inner life and rowed hard for the raft
where summer fun was waiting with its brawny cannonballs
and swan dives. I think each memory is lit
by its own small moon – a snowberry,
a mothball, a dime – which regulates its tides
and longings. Next time I am going to lift the oars
so we can watch the droplets fall back,
hidden ocean into unknown ocean,
while we drift. I will need a word
to float there, some empty blue-green bottle
that has lost its label. When we lose the trail entirely,
or it feeds us to the rain forest,
what will we be like? Probably not the Winter Wren,
whose impossible song is the biography of Buddha,
then Mary Shelley, then your no-good Uncle Ray.
Not the Cat-tail Moss
which hangs in drapes and furs the fallen logs in lavish
sixties shag. I think we come here so our words
can fail us, get humbled by the stones, drown,
be lost forever, then come back
as beach glass, polished and anonymous,
knowing everything. Knowing everything they
think of has already happened, everything they think of has
already happened and been sung, knowing
everything they think of has already happened and been sung,
in all its tongues and metres, and to no one,
by the sea.

NORTHERN LIGHTS

(October: Muenster, Saskatchewan)

We had outwalked the abbey's modest halo,
the under-hum of ritual, the monks like sleeping bees,
to face north with its cold
neurological laughter. Underfoot the frost
crisp in the grass, overhead
shafts and scarves that rippled and
unrippled in faint glacial aqua, something dangerous,
radioactive, light that has strayed so far it's
lost touch with its first
catastrophe, light with no reference to heat,
no family tie with reason.
I thought of moonlight,
doling out illusion like a medicine
month after month, how there are other madnesses
immune to myth, jokes we don't get.
We might as well be insects
waking to our final metamorphosis, old
and fresh at once, unable to tell which selves are the moths,
which the chimerae,
                           which the ghosts.
It would not have surprised me then to meet
some member of the dead, perhaps the one
who ran off with the dog, or the one who still lives
as a wounded bird under the porch – to meet
and mingle, one cloud of charged particles
passing through another,
and passing on.

THE BOOK OF MOONLIGHT

"The book of moonlight is not written yet."
  – Wallace Stevens

Arriviste, you are the reader
who has come too early, or too late,
and lingers in the spill of light
which might be aftermath, might be
anticipation. Plots that once were
furtive among leaves have long since
hatched from narrative into a sort of
disembodied drinking, a long-distance runner smoothly
shedding feet as she grows more and more
mercurial. How about you? Will you also shed the wish
not to be mistaken as your breath flits
in and out among the rumours and the cat
follows its whiskers into pure nuance?
In the scene you've missed, or are
about to witness, desire
and departure rendezvous. No hero happens,
unless it is you, the creature at the cusp of change,
the avid unabashed *voyeur.*

WINTER SOLSTICE MOON: AN ECLOGUE

(December: Pacific Rim National Park)

Full moon falling on Christmas Eve: I wondered,
as we carried our supplies – wine, rain gear, gifts –
from the car to the cabin, whether everything was
about to get conscripted into either family life
or lunacy. We put
the perishables in the fridge,
walked out on the beach: in the east
the blacker blackness of the mountains, already backlit
by the moon, and lower down each cabin's roof
outlined in lights, reminding everyone that this
was supposed to be the feast of homes
and homebodies, the time to bring a tree indoors
and charm its boreal heart with bric-a-brac,
to make ourselves so interesting its needles would forget
the roots they left behind. On the wet
corrugated sand the lights were smeared and
rippled, an elaborate film noir effect,
an opening sequence into which a cop car,
like an urban orca, should intrude. To the west
ocean was a far roar under its hush-hush
on the sand, a giant with a lisp.

I was thinking of the house we'd left
huddled darkly round its
turned-down furnace, one missing tooth
in the block's electric smile. How much

we ask of them, that they articulate
the space around us into stanzas,
pauses in the flow which gather time,
or rather, where time, slightly pregnant,
might gather if it chose; that they should be the bodies
of our bodies and the spirit's husk
against the hypothermia which dogs it,
a.k.a. the dreads; that they be resolute yet intimate, insulated,
pest-free, dry, well-founded in the earth but airy,
fire in the belly and a good deep well attached to copper
plumbing, CSA approved; that they should be
possessed of character but not by ghosts, and not
the sort of character who wakes you
in the middle of the night and suddenly
needs money; that they should shed the rain and keep the wind
from blowing out the candle flame of talk, the bedtime stories,
murmurings, the small redundant phrases with which one voice
solaces another.
And when it goes awry – the cracks the bills the noise the
drains the silences the bugs – to take the blame and sit there,
stoically, on the market while new dreamers sniff the air
and poke their noses into closets,
hatching their improbable plots.

We walked through soft mist,
filling our ears with the ocean's boom
and whisper. Is it the listening that loosens,
letting its knots go, or the voice,
saying those great unsayings to itself until
ovation on the inside equals ovation out? And rain forest,
I thought as we turned back at the cliff,

must be the way it gets translated into plants,
who remember water with each rounded,
downward gesture.
                    Then the moon. Over the mountain it hung
and roiled inside itself,
pure style which took the scene aslant, selecting
the bristle of frost on the drift logs, the patch
of duct tape on my boot, the whites of your eyes,
leaving whatever was not glimmering in deeper shadow,
uninhabited. Can you recall
those nights we spent learning from the wolves to be
the tooth and tongue of darkness, how to hunt
and howl? Me neither. Now that howl's
inverted in us, the long *o* of *alone*. The wolves
are dogs. The sun says *here*, the moon says
nowhere, the nameless moon
that sheds the blunt domesticating myths
the way a mirror utterly forgets you
when you leave the bathroom, the empty moon
soliciting our ghosts, calling on them to leave home,
that gilded cage, that theme park of the human.

But the sea was gazing back, its look
rich with tumult and the possibility of huge hearts
sounding the depths. Between them
otherworldliness is quickened. One theory –
my favourite – goes that once the earth and moon were one,
spinning monthlessly in space, and somehow – whether by asteroid
or apple, *différance*, tabu – they broke up and the moon,
newly fallen, risen, floated off into its orbit, while
into the crater of its absence flowed

the great tear known as the Pacific Ocean.

So:

a story full of loss and eros, three-fifths
of the way to myth. Let's leave it there – something human,
homespun, like a basket, a translation, or a loaf of bread –
beside the incandescent water. Our cabin sat
under its little party hat of lights, and to it,
wanting its warmth, and supper, and to give our gifts,
we went.

ON LEAVING

"Leaving home is the beginning of resemblance."
    – David Seymour

On leaving, you circulate among the things you own
to say farewell, properly,
knowing they will not cease to exist
after your departure, but go,
slowly, each in its own way,
wild.
So long and thanks, with one last chop, tap,
twiddle. It won't work just to
flip them into negatives – minus T-shirt, minus Roger
Tory Peterson both east and west –
nor to convert them into liquid
assets. This is no yard sale, this is loss,
whose interior is larger than its shell, the way you wish
home was. Do not dig the dog's bones up
nor the rosebush by the porch.
Choose a few companions of no weight –
a crow feather found in the parking lot,
the strawsmell of her hair, a few
books of the dead, *1000*
Best Loved Puns. And leave. There is a loneliness
which must be entered rather than resolved, the moon's
pull on the roof which made those asphalt shingles
shine. A time for this,
a time for that, a time to let them both escape into
whateverness, a time to cast

away stones, to stop
building and remembering and building artful
monuments upon the memories.

                                      To leave.
To step off into darker darkness,
that no moon we call new.

ACKNOWLEDGEMENTS

Some of these poems have appeared in *The Fiddlehead, Event,* and *The Malahat Review,* as well as in chapbooks from Reference West, Outlaw Editions, and Trout Lily Press. Some were commissioned and broadcast by the CBC under the title "Aria." My thanks to all the editors involved.

"Wings of Song" is dedicated to Stan Dragland.

"Finger Pointing at the Moon" is in memory of Jane Clement Chamberlin, 1945-1998.

The epigraph to "Leaving Home" comes from an early draft of David Seymour's poem "Movement Is the Beginning."

Over the years I have benefited immensely from the ears of fine readers, among them Stan Dragland, Kim Maltman, Robert Bringhurst, Tim Lilburn, Dennis Lee, and Jan Zwicky. With this book, I am especially indebted to my editor, Roo Borson, for devoting such close, sharp-eared attention to the poems.

This book is for Jan Zwicky.